TRICERATOPS

REVISED EDITION

A TRUE BOOK®

by
Elaine Landau

Children's Press®
A Division of Scholastic Inc.

New York Toronto London Auckland Sydney
Mexico City New Delhi Hong Kong
Danbury, Connecticut

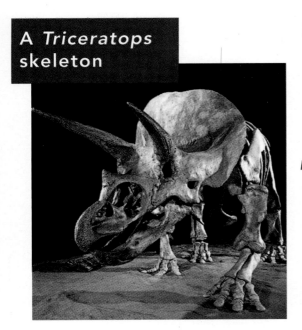

A *Triceratops* skeleton

Content Consultant
Susan H. Gray, MS, Zoology,
Little Rock, Arkansas

Reading Consultant
Cecilia Minden-Cupp, PhD
Former Director, Language and
Literacy Program
Harvard Graduate School of
Education

Author's Dedication
For Ava

*The photograph on the cover
and the title page shows a
model of Triceratops.*

Library of Congress Cataloging-in-Publication Data
Landau, Elaine.
    Triceratops / by Elaine Landau. — Rev. ed.
        p. cm. — (A true book)
    Includes bibliographical references and index.
    ISBN-10: 0-531-16831-X (lib. bdg.)   0-531-15471-8 (pbk.)
    ISBN-13: 978-0-531-16831-8 (lib. bdg.)   978-0-531-15471-7 (pbk.)
    1. Triceratops—Juvenile literature. I. Title. II. Series.
QE862.O65L355 2007
567.915'8—dc22
                                                            2006004425

CHILDREN'S PRESS, and A TRUE BOOK™, and associated logos are
trademarks and/or registered trademarks of Scholastic Library Publishing.
SCHOLASTIC and associated logos are trademarks and/or registered
trademarks of Scholastic Inc.
1 2 3 4 5 6 7 8 9 10 R 16 15 14 13 12 11 10 09 08 07

Contents

The three horns of *Triceratops* make it easy to see how this dinosaur got its name.

At the Start

Imagine that you have traveled back in time to the Age of the Dinosaurs. Luckily, you do not have to wait long to see one. Looking around, you see a large dinosaur headed your way.

This huge, leathery-skinned **reptile** is about 30 feet

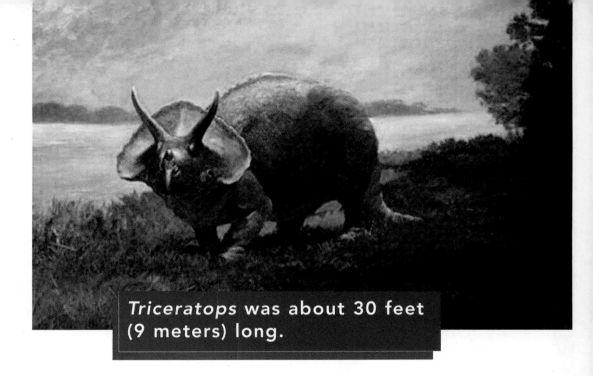

Triceratops was about 30 feet (9 meters) long.

(9 meters) long. That is about as long as a medium-sized school bus. Yet *Triceratops*'s head is what catches your eye. The dinosaur's head is about 6 feet (1.8 m) long, or about the size of a tall man.

You are starting to feel a little nervous. You wonder when this

Same Place, Different Time

*T*riceratops roamed the earth between 65 million and 70 million years ago. *Triceratops* lived during a time known as the Age of the Dinosaurs. The earth was warmer then. There were no cold seasons. Grass did not exist yet. Instead, a blanket of green ferns and other low-growing plants covered the ground. This was the world of *Triceratops*.

Earth during the time of *Triceratops* was very different from today's world.

dinosaur had its last meal. There is no need to worry, though. This huge creature eats only plants, so you are safe. You have just seen the dinosaur called *Triceratops*.

Triceratops ate plants that grew close to the ground.

A Closer View of *Triceratops*

Have you ever seen a rhinoceros? *Triceratops* looked like a very big rhinoceros. It had strong shoulders and a body shaped like a barrel. *Triceratops* had a short tail. It also had horns on its face.

Triceratops was much bigger than a rhinoceros, though. The heaviest rhinoceros weighs less than 3 tons. A full-grown *Triceratops* could weigh as much as 12 tons. It was like a living army tank.

Four sturdy legs supported this dinosaur's large body. Its hind, or back, legs were longer than its front legs. Its short front legs were quite strong, however. Powerful front legs helped support

Triceratops looked like a rhinoceros (above), only much bigger.

Triceratops's huge head. Its head weighed about 400 pounds (181 kilograms)! This is as much as a male gorilla.

Triceratops means "three-horned face." You could not miss the horns on this dinosaur's face. A short, thick horn rested just above its snout, which was shaped like a bird's beak. Two larger horns jutted out from above its eyes. These sharp horns were about 3 feet (almost 1 m)

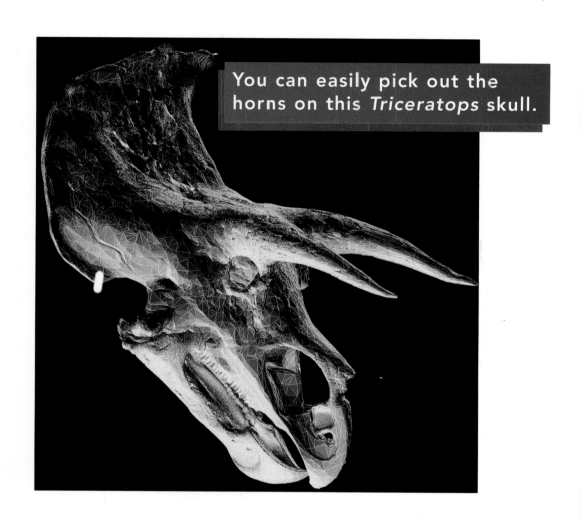

You can easily pick out the horns on this *Triceratops* skull.

long, or about the length of a hockey stick.

A large, fan-shaped plate of bone circled the back of this dinosaur's head. It was called a **frill**. On an adult *Triceratops*, the frill might be 7 feet (2 m) wide. Along the frill's outer edge was usually a row of small, pointed, knob-shaped bones.

Paleontologists—scientists who study **prehistoric** life—think that *Triceratops* may have used its bony frill as a weapon or a shield. It would

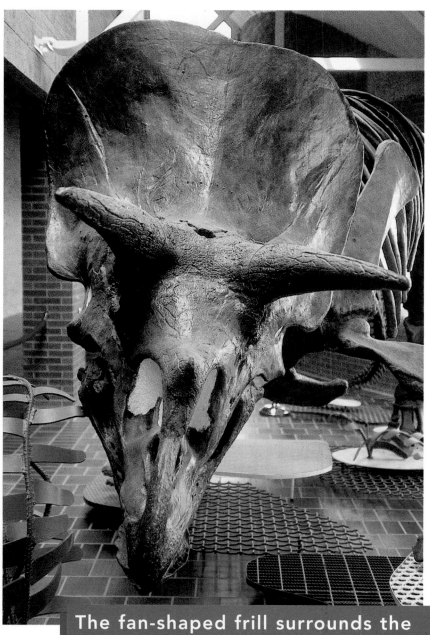
The fan-shaped frill surrounds the head of this *Triceratops* skeleton.

have been useful when other dinosaurs attacked. Or *Triceratops* may have displayed its frill to attract a mate. The dinosaur would have lowered its head to show how big its frill was.

Triceratops was an impressive animal. It belonged to a family of dinosaurs called ceratopsids. The ceratopsids had huge heads, bony neck frills, and horns. *Triceratops* was among the largest of the ceratopsids.

Styracosaurus, which looked a lot like *Triceratops*, belonged to the ceratopsid family.

Triceratops's head was positioned low on its body so it could graze easily.

How Triceratops Lived

Triceratops was an herbivore, or plant eater. However, it left the leaves on the taller trees to the long-necked dinosaurs. *Triceratops* ate the plants and bushes that grew closer to the ground. It may have used its horns to snatch up clumps of leaves and branches to eat.

During the time that *Triceratops* lived, flowering plants and trees were beginning to appear on the earth. These flowering plants and trees were called angiosperms. It is likely that *Triceratops* ate a great deal of these angiosperms.

This dinosaur had strong jaw muscles and tightly packed rows of teeth. Its teeth were not good for chewing. They worked like scissors instead. *Triceratops* used them to cut off chunks of plants that it swallowed whole.

This fossil of a *Triceratops* jawbone shows the dinosaur's teeth.

Triceratops must have had a powerful digestive system to handle all that unchewed food. Today's reptiles do not chew their food either. Like *Triceratops*, they swallow their food whole and digest it slowly.

Triceratops was always on the lookout for food. These dinosaurs roamed the land searching for rich, green areas. Some scientists think that they might have traveled

Triceratops may have traveled in herds.

in groups called herds. This would have provided some protection against **predators**.

Meat-eating dinosaurs would probably have been less likely to attack an entire herd. However, *Triceratops* was not defenseless. Its horns may have been excellent

weapons. The horns could stab a predator. *Triceratops* also may have used its horns to fight other *Triceratops* over food or areas where they roamed.

A *Triceratops* herd prepares to fight off a *Tyrannosaurus rex*.

Fossils: Bringing the Past to Life

Much of what we know today about dinosaurs comes from studying **fossils**. Fossils are evidence of plants and animals that lived long ago. Fossils might include bones, footprints, teeth, or leaf imprints on rocks.

A paleontologist studies a *Triceratops* horn.

Most fossils are uncovered through erosion. Erosion occurs when water and wind wear down the rock and expose the buried fossils.

In rare cases, mining or construction projects have blasted apart rocks and exposed fossils.

Over the years, paleontologists have found *Triceratops* fossils in Montana, North Dakota, South Dakota, and Wyoming. (*Triceratops* has even been named the state dinosaur of Wyoming.) Fossils have also been discovered in Alberta and Saskatchewan, Canada.

This map shows areas where *Triceratops* fossils have been found.

About fifty *Triceratops* skulls have been uncovered. Other fossil parts of this dinosaur have been found as well. These fossils give paleontologists a better idea of how the prehistoric creatures looked and lived.

A paleontologist works to uncover the fossil of a horned dinosaur.

These dinosaur tracks are millions of years old.

Paleontologists also learn about dinosaur behavior through fossil footprints. These are formed when a prehistoric animal leaves a footprint in the mud. Over a very long time, the mud hardens into rock. Paleontologists have found out a lot about *Triceratops* through fossil footprints. Such footprints have shown paleontologists that groups of these dinosaurs often walked together. That is why they think that *Triceratops* lived and traveled in herds.

Some of the fossil footprints show small footprints, with large footprints around them. Paleontologists think

A Funny Fossil Mistake

Othniel Charles Marsh found horns, like these from *Triceratops*. He thought they belonged to a bison.

The first *Triceratops* fossil ever found was a set of horns that stuck out from above the eyes. The paleontologist Othniel Charles Marsh examined the fossil in 1887. He thought that the horns belonged to an ancient bison. He did not learn until two years later that the horns belonged to a dinosaur.

that the young stayed in the center of the group. Adults surrounded the young to protect them from predators.

Paleontologists use computers to help them learn more about dinosaurs. After the paleontologists measure fossils, the measurements are used to make computer models of *Triceratops* and other dinosaurs. Computer models help paleontologists see how different kinds of dinosaurs moved.

Computer models were used to create this picture of *Triceratops*.

For about 180 million years, many kinds of dinosaurs and other reptiles lived on Earth.

Extinct! Going, Going, Gone

All dinosaurs did not become extinct, or die out completely, at the same time. For about 180 million years, various kinds of dinosaurs existed. Yet no single type of dinosaur lasted the entire time.

At the end of the Age of the Dinosaurs, all the remaining dinosaurs died out. Even this did not happen in one day. It took about one million

This timeline of prehistoric Earth shows when *Triceratops* lived.

	Triassic period		Jurassic period	
245 Million years ago	225 m.y.a. First dinosaurs appeared	208 m.y.a.	Many dinosaurs and first birds existed	144 m.y.a.

years for all the dinosaurs to disappear.

There is no definite answer as to why the dinosaurs became extinct. Many scientists think

(Note:"m.y.a." means "million years ago")

Cretaceous period | Tertiary period

70-65
m.y.a.
Triceratops
existed

65
m.y.a.
Last dinosaurs
became extinct

1.6
m.y.a.
First humans
appeared

that the dinosaurs became extinct after an asteroid crashed into Earth. Asteroids are large, rocky, planetlike bodies that move through space. If an asteroid struck Earth, a huge crater, or hole, would have been created.

The dust from the hole would have floated up into the **atmosphere** to form thick, dark clouds. These clouds would have blocked out the sun. The earth would have

Many paleontologists believe dinosaurs died out after an asteroid crashed into Earth.

become very cold. The dinosaurs probably could not have survived the cold temperatures.

During the Age of the Dinosaurs, Earth was still changing. The large landmasses called

The head of this *Triceratops* skeleton looks huge next to these children.

continents had not finished forming. Seas and mountain ranges were still taking shape. Different kinds of plant life appeared. The dinosaurs probably were unable to get used to all these changes.

Triceratops was one of the last dinosaurs to roam the earth. Although *Triceratops* will never wander Earth again, fossil discoveries help us learn more about this three-horned dinosaur.

To Find Out More

Here are some additional resources to help you learn more about *Triceratops*:

 **Books**

Dalla Vecchia, Fabio Marco. **Triceratops**. Blackbirch, 2004.

Gray, Susan H. **Triceratops**. Child's World, 2004.

Matthews, Rupert. **Triceratops**. Heinemann, 2003.

Skrepnick, Michael. **Triceratops: Mighty Three-Horned Dinosaur**. Enslow, 2005.

Theodorou, Rod. **I Wonder Why Triceratops Had Three Horns and Other Questions About Dinosaurs**. Kingfisher, 2003.

Organizations and Online Sites

The Dinosauria
http://www.ucmp.berkeley.edu/diapsids/dinosaur.html

Check out this Web site for some great dinosaur information. Be sure to read the answers to some of the most commonly asked dinosaur questions.

National Museum of Natural History—Dinosaur Exhibits
http://www.nmnh.si.edu/paleo/dino/trinew.htm

Visit this site for an up-close view of the museum's terrific *Triceratops* exhibit.

Project Exploration
950 East 61st Street
Chicago, IL 60637
http://www.info@projectexploration.org

This organization works to increase students' interest in paleontology.

Important Words

atmosphere the blanket of gases that surrounds Earth

fossils evidence of plants and animals that lived long ago. Fossils might include bones, footprints, teeth, or leaf imprints on rocks.

frill a large bony plate that stretches out from the back of a dinosaur's skull

predators animals that hunt other animals for food

prehistoric from the time before history was recorded

reptile a cold-blooded animal that crawls on the ground or creeps on short legs

Index

Meet the Author

Award-winning author Elaine Landau worked as a newspaper reporter, an editor, and a youth-services librarian before becoming a full-time writer. She has written more than 250 nonfiction books for young people, including True Books on animals, countries, and food. Ms. Landau has a bachelor's degree in English and journalism from New York University as well as a master's degree in library and information science. She lives with her husband and son in Miami, Florida.